Worth the Candle

Worth the Candle

poems by
Gary Glauber

Five Oaks Press
FIVE-OAKS-PRESS.COM

Copyright ©2017 Gary Glauber
All rights reserved. First print edition.

Five Oaks Press
Newburgh, NY 12550
five-oaks-press.com
editor@five-oaks-press.com

ISBN: 978-1-944355-27-2

Cover Photo: Rewat Wannasuk, used under Creative Commons Zero license and modified from the original.
Book Cover Design: Domenico Petrillo
Author Photo: Domenico Petrillo

Printed in the United States of America

Acknowledgments

Many thanks to the kind editors of the following journals in which these poems first appeared:

3 Elements Review: "None the Wiser"
Brickplight: "Queen of Period Eight"
Chupa Cabra House: "Alcmene's Dilemma"
Dead Flowers: "Tribal Rite"
Deep Water Literary Journal: "Putrid Deliquescence," "In Philippa's Hands," "Jeremiad"
Dirty Chai: "Welcome to the New Times"
Diverse Voices Quarterly: "An Octave Apart"
East Jasmine Review: "Evolution"
Emerge Literary Journal: "The Problem with Solving Problems"
Eunoia Review: "Not for Us," "Signal Chain"
Extract(s): "Onset"
Fjords Review: "Graveyard Shift"
Flutter Poetry Journal: "Look Before"
Foliate Oak Literary Magazine: "Migration," "Campaign Kiss," "Simile," "Party Favors"
Ginger Piglet: "Prophet"
Gravel: "Surmising the Situation," "Music Teacher," "Gala"
Heavy Feather Review: "The Dispassionate Punishment," "Sidereal Splendor," "Found and Lost"
Indian Summer Quarterly: "Submerged"
JMWW: "In the Barn"
Kindred Magazine: "Hard Cycle"
Meat for Tea: The Valley Review: "King of Aces," "Underpass"
Noctua Review: "Solitaire"
Northwind Magazine: "Portrait"
OVS: "Controlled Procedure"
Ozone Park Journal: "Seasons of Loss"
Panoply: "Anagnorisis"
Petrichor Review: "Off Ramp"

Poemeleon: "The Mix-Up"
Red Ochre Lit: "The Trouble is One of Style," "Liquidators"
Red Poppy Review: "Regular"
Sheila-Na-Gig: "The Calculating"
Sparkbright Magazine: "Reins"
Stone Voices: "The Rising," "Fresh-Brewed Fog"
Stoneboat Journal: "Illuminated"
Tendril Literary Magazine: "Neighborly Act," "Lex Loci"
The Bicycle Review: "Modern Romance"
The Blue Hour Magazine: "Reconnaissance," "Back to School," "Invasive"
The Bookends Review: "Hawk Versus Crow"
The Chaffin Journal: "Feathered Thing"
The Citron Review: "Anthem," "Refrain"
The Courtship of Winds: "Unnatural Law"
The Kitchen Poet: "Play"
The Legendary: "Greatest Fan"
Thin Air Magazine: "The Reveal"
Think Journal: "Happenstance"
Thirteen Myna Birds: "Acts of Nature"
Tilt-a-Whirl: "Second Act"
Twisted Vine Literary Arts Journal: "Unscheduled"
Typoetic.us: "Deluminate"

Contents

Long ago, candles were so costly that activities needed to justify the expense of creating enough light to partake in them.

I. Semblances

Welcome to the New Times	7
Portrait	8
Neighborly Act	9
Tribal Rite	10
Alcmene's Dilemma	11
Fresh-Brewed Fog	13
Modern Romance	15
Unscheduled	17
Sidereal Splendor	18
Off-Ramp	19
The Problem with Solving Problems	20
Reminder	21
Acts of Nature	23
The Calculating	24
In Philippa's Hands	25

II. Chronicles

Tribute	29
Putrid Deliquescence	30
Hawk Versus Crow	31
Regular	32
Controlled Procedure	33
The Rising	34
Found and Lost	35
Liquidators	36
The Dispassionate Punishment	37
Look Before	38
The Trouble Is One of Style	39
Graveyard Shift	40
Campaign Kiss	41
Music Teacher	42

Solitaire	43
In the Barn	45
The Mix-Up	46
King of Aces	48
Jeremiad	50

III. Assorted Wicks

Play	53
Anthem	54
Deluminate	55
Refrain	56
Simile	57
Prognosis	58
Signal Chain	59
Migration	60
Gala	61
Feathered Thing	62
An Octave Apart	63
Stasis	64
None the Wiser	65
Reconnaissance	67
Evolution	68
Onset	69
Hard Cycle	70
Surmising the Situation	71
The Reveal	72
Party Favors	73
Illuminated	74

IV. Shadow Tricks

Invasive	77
Seasons of Loss	78
Back to School	79
Happenstance	81
Not for Us	82
Unnatural Law	84
Prophet	85
Anagnorisis	86
Second Act	87
Lex Loci	89
Submerged	90

Underpass	91
Reins	92
Queen of Period Eight	93
Greatest Fan	94

*For Deborah, Zane, and Graham,
with love and gratitude*

I. Semblances

Welcome to the New Times

At one time, every little doodad
needed inventing.
Now people lack the requisite patience
to do that kind of constant attempting,
to stay up all hours trying this, that,
and the infamous other thing.
There are no wizards in waiting;
they have all been replaced
by less ambitious basement dwellers,
gamers, and sundry self-promoters.
So as society sits in the dark,
hoping for thingamajigs
of practical cleverness that
might ease the way to the next
burgeoning idea revolution,
the only dim lights seen
are cell-phone photo flashes,
artless selfies of
our own contented despair.

Portrait

You were the woman crouched
back in the lower acres of the meadow,
under the umbrella of that distant elm,
a yellow skirt fluttering in the balmy breeze,
a bushel of threshed grain collected
as your prize, your set piece,
the landscape's silent focal point.

You were its punishment,
as well as its peace rewarded,
a soul aligned with its environs,
remote from the politics that attend
our daily chores here, the painful
naked honesty of our respective labors.
Someday you'll be some child's mother,
but in this moment's particular freedom,
your eager smile conveys youthful instinct,
an innocent faith that has yet to learn
the ravages of unpainted time,
the raw truths that art cannot capture.

Neighborly Act

The fact that she lives
on another continent
doesn't stop her from berating me.
I was peeling a carrot,
raising a child,
completing a domestic task.
She said she saw me through the window.
She took off her hat.
She had an accent, but she knew my name.
I listened, hoping for an explanation.
Her clothes were the same colors
as the ones I was wearing.
Still, no secret meaning was revealed.
I excused myself, fed the fish,
and when I returned
she had rearranged the furniture
into some kind of labyrinth.
I was impressed, yet felt badly
for the friends I was expecting later that day.
No one would recognize the place now.
She mumbled something about an ancient custom,
then quietly snuck out of my life.

Tribal Rite

You decide to kiss me
passionately
in the hallway of the Native American artifacts,
right in front of a crowd of inanimate warriors
who people the display case to our left.
They circle the fire and
seem to mind their own business.
I like how you waited until
that bunch of bored school kids
moved quickly along to something
they hoped might prove more exciting.
They would never know
the folly of their impatience.
For you like the intimacy of the public space,
the idea of the unexpected.
You grab my attention and more,
and while the guard in the next room
daydreams about some upcoming vacation,
you make my history come alive now.

Alcmene's Dilemma

In hindsight, she recalls it seemed unusual.
Amphitryon was a good man, but not the kind
who could go at it twice in one night,
and certainly not with such impressive passion.
It seemed strange even during
those first throes of wanton desire.

That first time, late in the afternoon,
when he almost forced himself upon her,
not speaking, not kissing, very unlike
the ritual coupling that had been borne
of years of marital familiarity, the known
dance that saved time and needless effort.

This new behavior had made her wonder
if he had been with another, some cheap
concubine who sold her wares and preferred
rough trade to tenderness, what with it
being a strumpet's business, and
fast and furious providing far greater profits.

Yet she allowed it then, discounting it
as sexual whimsy, a fiery mood, and riding along
to feed the ravages of a starving man.
She noted the lack of sweat, even amidst
the sustained physical exertion of the task.
Oddly, he then excused himself, returning to work.

Later that night he was more like himself,
full of the market's gossip and eager to share,
stopping to assure for her pleasure first,
the true gentleman she had always loved:
kind, caring, generous, compassionate.
The man she desired still, after years together.

She was at the height of fertility that day,
as the months to follow revealed,
and when she gave birth to twins

the following Spring, she never gave
that doubly passionate occasion
even a hint of second thought.

But now that Heracles and Iphicles
are grown to be quite different boys,
both in appearance and behavior,
she went to consult the ancient oracle,
to better understand how brothers
of the same womb can be so unalike.

It spoke strange words:
heteropaternal superfecundation,
and then she started to remember
about the two times of arduous coupling.
That first time had not been her husband at all,
but another of the god Zeus' clever disguises.

So now she has given birth
to twin sons of separate fathers,
and must never favor one over the other.
And while one is a paragon of extraordinary strength,
courage, ingenuity, and male sexual prowess,
the other likes to sit around and mope.

This is hard, she thinks, and unfair.
Let this be a lesson to others,
she writes in her secret diary.
When something out of the ordinary
enters the realm of marital lovemaking,
be suspicious indeed, and try hard to resist.

Fresh-Brewed Fog

Those ancient commercials conveyed
the anxiety of small-town bean growers,
facing the test of purchase and scrutiny
from "El Exigente," the demanding one,
he whose discerning mustachioed judgment
decided so much in the name of Savarin coffee.
These days our coffee judgments
involve no travel by burro to distant regions;
today we argue about where to congregate
over a French-roasted Kona brew
with flavor strong enough to approximate
similar Arabica or Colombian offerings.
Should it be that local corner shop
where chatty divorcees gather
to drown recent aggravations
and fashion compromised concerns
into a dream for a fun weekend ahead?
Should it be that nationally branded Seattle-chain
where less-than-comfy furniture
attracts local vagabonds and colorful characters
like flies to summer garbage?
We shall make our choice and
place our orders, then sit and sip
and talk for an hour, venting
over our ventis, raging against
the dying of the light, or more likely
against the petty concerns that occupy
our postmodern humdrum lives,
having elevated ambiguity into art
or a commercial for said art instead.
We couch fears in measured cups
of caffeinated beverages
that prove Eliot's insights
when watching lonely men and women.
Yes, we know them all,
and if you listen closely to all the
Samsara chattering surrounding us,
one can even imagine them as lyrics

to a universal song that one day
will liberate, will deliberate,
will gnash and churn and agonize
toward an end of human harmony.

Modern Romance

From the relative safety of this parapet,
he sees gray raindrops fall,
slipping down the million black umbrellas
of the common majority. For a second
he envisions it is an army come to free him
from his current burden, the strife
of a gentleman's wrongheaded resolve,
a sentence of a lifetime of days alone,
furious at being a prisoner in the tower,
with sporadic internet service at best.

She rides the escalator upward
to that familiar third floor department
past racks full of cotton nighties
and more conservative flannel offerings.
She finds what she wants beyond that,
a flimsy lace teddy, something else silken
and scanty, the soft wares that her body
fills to alluring perfection. The genetic
gifts she inherited are best seen through
such thin coverings as these, and as she
carries today's handful to the changing room,
she also knows that these things exist
beyond the ken of her minimum wage earnings.
Still, she changes into each suggestive outfit in turn,
and snaps a few expert poses, digital camera
held off to the mirror's side. Megapixels
capture the images well, sensual yearnings or
lustful longings to a world of imaginary admirers.

It doesn't take much to set him off lately:
the blare of car horns in a rush hour's entanglement,
the reminder from a lawyer that parole seems
a long shot, the reflection that greets him
off a shiny surface in passing. So this
downloaded vision of pulchritude is a
welcome respite, a momentary pardon of sorts,
a chance to imagine a fantasy of freedom

that takes him outside his celled existence
and into the waiting arms of this young angel
who insists she's legal. For now, the sound of rain
distracts him not, and he is less concerned with
details, other than those in the zoomed image
on the screen before him, lingerie modeled
so sweetly it must be love.

Unscheduled

That woman in Edinburgh,
hiding me in her dorm room,
in the literal shadows of a castle;
I was the night's
mysterious contraband.

Subjecting me as well to her love
of Europop, its insipid lightness,
giving me her restless body
to harmonic rhythms of those
mocking bubblegum sounds,
surrendering awkwardness into
slap and tickle, the desperate act
of the young and lonely.

The note board on her door
exhibited a few hastily doodled flowers.
There was an open can of diet cola
on a small bedside table.

I remember the spare settings,
her embarrassed apologies
early the next morning,
as she hurriedly conducted me
through narrow hallways,
eager to get me out undiscovered.

Soon I was liberated into
the coolness of empty streets,
given no way to find her, to express
this strange tourist's gratitude.

Sidereal Splendor

I still smell the cut grass in her spacious backyard
that long summer day, the various booths and rides
set up to raise funds for some worthwhile cause
that escapes me. I was first in line to purchase tickets
that afforded access to that wet and wild slippery slide,
where her freckled shenanigans brought a giggling glow
to the proceedings, enticing me back again and again.
When she moved to the far booth, I followed.
While hoops never landed in a way to earn me a prize,
being around her then was reward enough.
We never confessed what was felt,
settling for a sociable familiarity, shared laughter,
the silliness of happy unexpressed urges.
I would visit her older obnoxious brother,
though that often ended poorly -- fistfights on the lawn.
These many decades later I confess to a silent world
how I stopped by merely to catch a glimpse,
to share a smile, to fuel my muted
and misunderstood adolescent dreams.
I expect she found a healthy balance
of career and family.
Now, in long nights of winter, I gaze heavenward
at celestial freckles blinking blankly
and ponder what is and what could have been,
ignoring lifetimes that have passed
to stop and ask,
What's a neighbor for?

Off-Ramp

He returns to revisit old haunts,
eager to measure how much remains
of that remembered magic,
but the discovery is this:
settings change and even a distant sunset
over the reservoir's wide horizon
retains none of the charm and *savoir faire*
experienced together that autumnal afternoon
when, after sharing anecdotal amusements,
she confessed all the reasons why
they could never be anything more
than a small footnote to a dream.
He had pleaded otherwise,
in a rare show of vulnerability,
but hadn't swayed her firm conviction.
Now a trifling tract house stands
where the billboard had been,
another disturbing reminder of suburbia.
Staring at the parade of cars and trucks
whizzing by the underpass,
he is struck by the insignificance
of what once loomed so large.
The bounding hum of their high-speed passing
is an echo that stretches toward infinity.
For life is a thruway, and further along,
exits become numbers, not places,
markers forging some larger journey.

The Problem with Solving Problems

The problem with solving problems
is that when the hours are in,
and appropriate formulae applied,
the calculations made and answers
double and triple checked,
it still doesn't change the facts
of this unforgiving economy,
that which cannot be fathomed.
Even smart and engaging candidates
have long odds in this equation,
particularly those seeking to land
any career-track position
without an insider's edge.
What is the sum of
doing more than what is asked
and getting no positive reward?
This short shrift society
is configured in ways that
defy logic, that rely on exceptions
to prove the rule, but very little
deviates from the frustrating standard.
And so, after hours of careful
solutions derived and recorded,
the larger problem still looms,
like Goldbach's conjecture,
or odd perfect numbers,
or more aptly, the elusive determination
of the smallest number
of points in a plane,
the happy ending problem.

Reminder

The visitor is grateful to deliver his message
to eager local denizens of this sunny suburban locale.
The library's community room is packed to the brim
with those whose youth has long since fled the scene.
There is a preponderance of black leather,
as if its presence could magically transport the wearer
back to when ponytails had a fuller, richer, darker hue,
when that late model Prius was
an impressively tripped-out hog.
Back then the Village had panache and presence,
and battles for love and free expression were set against
warmongers and a generation hell-bent on defense
from a red menace and a nuclear threat
that sent folks running to duck and cover.

The music was loud, the times so much simpler.
And now, this modest visitor, their contemporary,
was speaking choice words to trigger a panoply
of fond memories and sentimental expectations.
This keeper of the dreams harkened to another age
of black and white and dialed times, screen doors
through which ballgames could be heard and
summer conversations amplified across
plaintive backyards and crowded picnic tables.
The gathered now listen respectfully,
eager to hear humorous anecdotes,
prologue to the prosaic set pieces,
the published memoranda,
the explorations of what set marriages asunder,
what made us laugh and cry,
that which made us so ultimately human.

An appeal to the gods was ever poignant that day,
chiding them for judging our flaws and imperfections,
assuring they could never know us quite half as well
as this eloquent visitor seemed to,
this survivor through decades
of what those in attendance read as savory experiences

that ultimately added up to a unique life and,
like every life,
worth knowing in detail,
worth sharing en masse.

Acts of Nature

Boys fumble
with innocent convictions:
falling, stumbling upon
what gives them away,
a vacancy in their eyes
approaching the register,
eager to write their fictions,
name by name,
hour by hourly rate,
stealing hard knowledge,
professing love (when necessary),
sharing unkind lies
no one believes.
In the distance,
a coyote pack's yelps
cover the ugly violence
that the dark night obscures.

The Calculating

A little hole in the wall of a place,
five stools at the counter
and a magazine and news rack.
Each day the regulars would convene,
pick up their reserved racing forms
and start their notations, curious systems
with circles and symbols and odds,
a sort of personal calculus,
based on hunches and odds,
weather, breeding, trainers,
and the wisdom of a seasoned jockey.
Lonergin would kid about luck,
Devito would chomp on an unlit cigar,
Direnzo would engage Leon, the owner,
in some shared memory or another.
My job was to feign indifference,
to assume invisibility while also refilling
a coffee cup, providing some cake,
perhaps hitting the fountain for
an occasional celebratory egg cream.
I never knew anything more about them,
whether they had jobs, families, wives, children.
They in turn never asked anything more
than "Hey, how're y' doing?"
because it was never about me, but rather
about this busy place of temporary privacy,
a solidly packed tiny retail space
affording them the unlikely illusion
of infinite area, a place for contemplation
attentive to their needs, yet never nosy
enough to question their trifecta pick
on the fourth race that day at Aqueduct.

In Philippa's Hands

Bring your soul to the eye of the fire,
that was her invitation
full of danger and promise and conviction.
She was intense, dramatic,
imagining herself twisted on rocky shoals,
burning the ships that carry the gold,
changing the world with her forced relevance.
My soul is smoking, she assured me,
and the hatred of the ignorant seeks to destroy it.
Her language tires me after a time,
and I close my eyes, inhaling the vague scent
of yesterday's opium and medicinal weed,
and try to accept her perpetual state of siege.
This requires work, I know, and as I attempt
to make this relationship viable,
I again hear in my mind's ear
the echoes of her familiar treatise
on the impending zombie apocalypse.

II. Chronicles

Tribute

A warm breeze,
a sweet summer's afternoon,
These are the just deserts,
the small consolations
for a solitary visitor's
solemn approach.
Cumulus clouds float by,
silent observers to this visit
minus the invisible memories
adding meaning to this
charade of ritual gestures,
this dark granite reminder
of one that came,
forged a sloppy life,
and left too soon thereafter.

A name graces the stone
and over years differences fade,
anger and resentments,
petty politics of family and friends.
The tribunal of neighbors and colleagues
eager to pass damning judgments
stands silenced by passing breeze.

In the end, strangers all,
governed by shared illusion
of time managed and owned,
surrender their temporal distortion
of brutish ego and empty promises,
taking leave of this existence,
and sending souls aloft
to destinations imagined,
but never known.

Putrid Deliquescence

Ungodly carnage on the hill of death
serves as silent testament to what has transpired.
After those rhythmic hoofbeats play their retreat
and fade into footnote of some future history's tale,
we hitch up our rigs and head over grain fields
soaked in blood to offer up meager assistance in the effort
to haul the wounded to dry ground,
a place where hope might attend them.

The humble lot of us, village farmers, now assemble
as a motley brigade of tired cavalry,
dots on the grim slope,
standing ruefully among parts and bodies
already bound for eternity.
The mud mingles thickly with the many unburied,
as we search for answers and relief
from the carrion stench, a deluge that grows more powerful
with each inch of the late summer sun's
slow journey across afternoon sky.

Ugly vultures converge on the rotting feast
this earthly plain offers. They screech and flap
huge black wings with frightening grace,
red-necked pillagers of this misguided plight,
where young rebels charged and lost, now
scattered lifeless, sprawled, friendless, gone.
There's strange beauty in these casual postures
of violent death and lessons for the rest,
those who step gingerly through this maze
of yellow corn now blemished crimson
in this land of war's fresh dead.

Hawk Versus Crow

No one travels to this part of town anymore,
not since the 5:06 has been rerouted
and the filling station removed its pumps.

The sole radio station plays mostly static
cut with echoes of a distant broadcast,
the excitement of a local sporting contest.

Here it is all phantasmal and bleak.
I clearly hear the double screech overhead
and see proud brown wings flap in aerial attack.

Yet the underbird here, the smaller crow
caws loudly, like a chatty old woman
shouting out feats of raffish grandchildren.

This cackle draws an immediate response.
Black dots appear as if called out of thin air,
flying from distant branches to gather in force.

The twenty birds that populate the branches
of the early spring's bare maple tree
understand how there is comfort in numbers.

Here below things are barely intact.
Unpainted shutters blow in the stiff breeze,
a morse code of lonely abandon.

The hawk screeches in final protest,
then flies away, defeated for now,
but reserving the right to fight again.

Down here, there's far less promise.
Rumors say the schools will close soon
along with the remaining branch of the bank.

In this place, I crow and no one comes
to shake these surrounding branches,
to win this singular battle.

Regular

He sits alone,
studying sidewalk traffic
that bisects the large restaurant window.
Nothing of this daily bustle strikes him as profound.
The family at the next table watches him
eat his toast, sip his coffee, and he smiles
at how they instantly judge him.
His grizzled two-day-old beard,
his dark drab clothes make him someone
they recognize, a pesky eyesore they wish was invisible.
He glances at the morning tabloid's
headline-driven gossip masquerading as news.
He reads every third paragraph
and still knows the score. Names change;
stories do not. He lets loose an exasperated sigh,
unfolds some wilted bills from a worn clip
and leaves them beside unfinished remains of
a special that was quite ordinary.
The boy at the next table tries to catch his eye,
but he knows better than to allow that.
He'll pay the cashier near the door,
then escape into a world where
each day becomes another reckless journey,
an ongoing quest for meaning and respect.

Controlled Procedure

Surgeon as human being must rise to this challenge,
ignoring conflicting emotions. He loved her once,
years ago. She spurned that love. And today
she is one of three cases, an atherectomy.
He will push a blade on a catheter through her heart.
He will cut his way through this heart
he could not sway.
The irony is not wasted on him.
Life is full of paradoxes that defy credulity,
that illustrate karmic wheels spinning.
She will be mildly sedated, as he expels
their shared past from his mind.
Through clearing an opening, he gets closure.
For an instant, he still wishes
he could somehow be blindfolded,
kept in the dark safety of anonymity.
He steels himself with a last sip of strong coffee,
then pulls up a blue mask that hides nothing,
and pretends his mind is clear.

The Rising

As sun peeks out over the waves of distant horizon,
we lie here, incredulous that another glorious day
has dawned, oblivious yet to the range of possibilities
it holds, the chance for history in the making
or perhaps a quiet time of somber reflection,
running the gamut of earthly emotions or merely
a rivulet of trivial indices that trace a circuitous course
to nowhere. This tabula rasa awaits painter's brush,
child's breath, human touch, seer's vision,
poet's fancy, lover's embrace, critic's wrath.

We wipe sleep from our bleary dreamers' eyes and
roll over, eager yet gingerly prim in our soft approach
to confront this new morn, to shed warm blankets of
familiar thoughts and face this sentient dumbshow together.

Sweet day, show us the aegis of your agenda,
reveal secrets of each sublime second,
the marvels and mysteries, the warp and woof
of this string of raw moments, its unique components,
a vexing conundrum that living alone will translate,
will solve.

Beauty's blank promise shines down as if solace
to quiet our spirits, so far from forlorn. We smile,
acknowledging what words cannot capture, the pleasure
and rapture, the hope we still wear. And cloaked
in that knowledge, we set off into it, another day wiser
in all that we bear.

Found and Lost

She was pasted firmly in the past,
trivial footnote in a weather-beaten journal
gathering dust, unread on a high closet shelf,
a brief coupling that held sweet silk memories
between torrents of mood swings and accusations.
She wore jealousy and lace, foolishly believing
both might strengthen a shaky relationship.
It ended ugly, a paean to passion gone awry.
Today she found me, posted intentions to catch up
on a virtual wall, like unwanted graffiti, neon loud
and barely hiding the anger behind the message.
It has been nearly two decades since our pairing.
Sure I smile now, remembering the time her leg
brushed sexily against me while not a soul
at the crowded table even suspected a thing,
how she brought lovely to a room
like a wafting fragrance.
But she was temperamental, erratic, and
used to getting her way, spoiled in the way
that beauty affords certain privileges.
The hammer of online silence strikes hard.
I delete the posting, overriding a risk in curiosity
because between the lines is where games are played,
and while I can hear her imagined vociferous denial,
it's obvious that who she is has not changed.

Liquidators

These empty hallways are desolate.
As we stroll these ghost-laden barracks,
the footsteps echo a little too loudly.
Dark green shutters provide hard contrast
to the pasty off-white cinder block walls.

Years ago this place was a busy terminal
of organized human chaos labeled basic training,
a simmering stew of discipline, fear, and testosterone,
with wrestling odors of sweat and fresh paint.
The only redolence remaining is of
stale southern summer air, hanging sauna-like
in a slow torpor that leaves rings
under arms and across backs, reminders
of an atmosphere that once served as prelude
for service in distant jungles and deserts.

Some clipboard marks are made
after measuring, noting dimensions and layouts.
This place seems much the same as the other five,
but we're paid to take time to assess and determine,
regard what can possibly be salvaged, reused or retooled.
This shut-down government playground
might be some local factory's dream come true,
but in this slow growth economy, most likely
we'll sell what we can at auction and raze the remainder.

What few industrial clients seeking expansion
find their needs overseas in sweetened deals
of cheap materials and cheaper labor,
a new global solution. Meanwhile, we swat
lazy horseflies and restless mosquitoes
and continue to size the place up best we can,
pretending it's all meaningful,
as if this history mattered somehow
beyond the bargain basement realities
of our hefty task at hand.

The Dispassionate Punishment

The Virgin wears a flattering low-necked
form-fitting neon red garment that clings tightly
and flatters her very bounteous natural gifts.
Her halo rests firmly in place, as the painting
on the wall, its love triangle's participants
closing their eyes in passion's embrace,
are unable to see her hand raised to chastise
her godly charge, prone in her lap,
flailing somewhat, awaiting the blow.
She hides half in shadow, staring off in thoughts
entirely unrelated to the important task at hand.
Everyone acknowledges the blessings
of the feted miracle birth,
but none dare appreciate
the politic discipline necessary
in carefully raising another's child.

Look Before

It's not that he's afraid of heights per se,
more that he's afraid of himself,
the terrible things he might do
at this dangerous elevation,
looking over the rail,
that vast temptation,
seeing the tiny specks that are the vehicles,
their red taillights snaking their way across midtown.
This sea of teeming humanity
that seems antlike, industrious, and tolerable
from this great distance
is crying out to see him
extend his arms and fly
like some superhero
on an earth-saving mission
at least for those few moments
before reality would catch up
to the fantastical impulse
and ruin the thrill
in a harsh blast of self-destruction.
And so he resists,
politely moving back
through the glass sliders
off the balcony
and into the no-leap safety
of this inner sanctum,
a room with no views.

The Trouble Is One of Style

Your eclectic collection of hope chests
houses closetsful of dreams and guises,
the stylish masquerade of the poseur's parade
and silky objects of leaner desire.
These are the remnants of past lives,
ideas for quick fashion fortunes
right beside more earnest outfits
that suited a workday's endeavor.
These clothes betray a life of
forced variety, a realm of color
that tiptoes beyond the pale,
transforming pastels into
palettes so intimately intricate
they suggest a cleverness of wit.
There are patterns that
convey pastiches, tableaus
that hint at murky modesty,
and rich tapestries that
run contrary to the Spartan tone
of these other surroundings.
Fine taffetas and crepe-de-chine
suggest luxurious splendor,
sumptuous times in other places,
in the company of royals,
dancing a secret tango
when such gifts were commonplace
and lush brocades protected
against harsh winds outside ice palaces.
Sinister time has since stolen occasions
for bringing such items
back to an evening's light,
and this telling catalog of a wardrobe
lies in limbo, gathering dust
amidst mothballs and cedar,
silent testament to nostalgic memories
and a galaxy of sartorial expectations
that reached far and wide, each in its time,
now a motley pile of fabric and fabrications,
a host of distant visions unraveled.

Graveyard Shift

The vagrant tree sprite
meets the head misfit
far along aisle five,
next to a pyramid of cereal boxes
neatly stacked, cartoon eyes
all following the action carefully.
A compromise is made
before the checkout begins.
Righteousness counts as
one item here, and the scanner
rings up some organic
benevolent flair.
This is your ritual,
your misplaced metaphor,
the wreckage of your urbane
constellation, gone sadly awry
in an uncharted midnight sky,
searching for meaning
in this 24/7 universe.

Campaign Kiss

There's nothing worth wearing
unless it makes some statement.
Such are the words spat at us,
awaiting your command
here in the cramped press room
outside the cushy hotel's convention center.
This is not the deal anyone
had signed on for those long months prior,
when still we bathed in naïve beliefs
about one person able to make a difference.
Now it's all threats and attitudes,
smirks and Smirnov chasers,
and standing up to unseen enemies
that battle us and also lurk within.
Money is the problem,
and perhaps the answer too.
You wish this happy hour extended
well into the work week,
that you were back on the farm,
part and parcel of
that imaginary childhood
pulled out whenever convenient.
We are slaves to statistics,
tied to poll numbers and media trendings,
and while I'd like to believe your passion
when you unfold me in that tiny space,
I know you are driven by ulterior motives
no one else could ever fathom.
You bid us a staccato welcome
and send us on our respective ways,
working tables under this chandelier glare,
raking nuance from belief
in what some third-string reporter
will inevitably call progress.

Music Teacher

Oh to be sequestered in a practice room with you,
soundproofed against the world's horrible noises.
The space cries out for a sweet duet.
Oh for that perfect chance to play notes
that express passions inherent to my native land,
riffs that cannot be ignored,
where each staccato utterance forces a body to move,
willing slave to the rhythm.
Such music thrills, fills me within and without,
exciting and delighting.
Yet all I manage this dull afternoon
is a stultified assemblage of amateur sounds,
a bric-a-brac of awkwardness that conveys
nothing of what burns inside.
This stiff, metrical mess seems unpracticed, crude.
I play on, sliding down a steep declension
toward the edge of crestfallen.
No arpeggio flourish impresses
and nothing distinguishes
my allegro hopes and dreams.
No coda rescues me today, yet you continue to smile,
beautiful and unperturbed, a petite fortress of patience
and aural fortitude brought to bear.
For this and more, I urge my heart
to beat pianissimo, lest its jungle
timpani of adoration scare you away.
Like millions of others I barely walk erect,
yet you encourage me to work opposable thumbs
in vague expectation that one day
this stiff hodgepodge of embarrassing notes
will evolve into the fine art of lovely music.

Solitaire

Sometimes these lonely evenings seem a kind of limbo
where nothing connects, and everything seems guessed
at incorrectly, as if he were a pariah of sorts, a fashion
castaway so outside the realm of normal that it seems
as though his every out-of-touch effort is taken in vain,
a thing of no importance, with not very much at stake.

Television on, he pretends leftovers are hearty steak,
each bite a fool's state where he can ignore this limbo
in a semblance of dignity, somewhat along the same vein
of his usual fantasy of being a dignified, honored guest
at state affairs, uniform pants embroidered at the seams
in some accepted mode of socialite elitist fashion.

But illusions fade, and his mood sours after a fashion
when he admits the routine sad truths at stake
with each wasted year, a lifetime spent alone seems
ever more likely as he examines this pitiful limbo
he calls existence, how it got this way can't be guessed
at, bad enough at times to tempt opening a vein.

He ponders what wild unnamed wind spins fate's vane
toward this position, leaving him removed from fashion
and passion, in the depths of being an unwelcome guest
in his own home and sad soul, with everything at stake,
friends, love, his universe for a chance to trade limbo
for meaningful interaction, everything that seems

desirable and beyond his current situation, all that seems
distantly unattainable, a slim hope against hope in vain,
a dancer's way to wriggle out from under this limbo
bar above his head, choking him down in hellish fashion
unrelenting, indifferent to his wants, a hardened stake
driven into a harder heart beating or beaten. He guessed

this world would welcome him happily and he guessed
wrong. The reality of rejections in a hard world seems

to contradict best intentions. Where winners eat steak, he is stuck managing meager cheap morsels, no vain purpose behind choices, scant budget dictating fashion selections, as expenses grow in this nightmare limbo.

He never guessed unnoticed efforts would all be in vain, it seems this cruel world won't accept his strange fashion - a life held at stake through suspension in social limbo.

In the Barn

Some say it was inevitable.
After all, there's a curse upon them,
with all their various crises
bearing this out from year to year.
My theory involves the
bricks in the renovated house,
recycled from an insane asylum,
a cruel place from an earlier era.
What kind of bad karma
and time-released superstition
was captured inside those red
building stones and soon expressed
like a particularly viral toxin
upon the already tenuous
state of mental fragility
that was the remainder
of a painful divorce;
who can say?
Alcohol, drugs, errant bullets,
cancers, tumors, odd
transportation mishaps,
suicide and more
plague this modern Camelot's
extended family.
And so another footnote
is added to the long list,
another life taken
in untimely fashion,
another inexplicable event
that adds fuel to the
rumormongering masses,
shaking their collective heads.

The Mix-Up

She came over to the park bench where I was sitting,
waiting for the workday to end so I could watch
people file out of the busy courthouse.
She sat down and kissed me on the forehead.
"Hello Scotty," she said. "Ready for our date?"
I had never seen this woman before in my life.
"Hello Ann," I said, reading her necklace.
"Are you going to start with that again?" she said.
"You know that's not my name." I figured
it could have been a monogram of some sort.
"You know what it stands for," she told me.
"Actually never named?" I guessed. She smiled,
before stopping to reapply some deep red-hued lipstick.
"The vet says Dyson's going to be okay."
It was obviously good news.
"Thanks for taking care of that," she said.
I had no clue as to what she meant, but I smiled
and nodded my head thoughtfully.
"Quite strange weather lately," I offered.
"Have you ever seen such strong winds?"
She said it reminded her of the time we
were at Punta Cana, at the height of hurricane season.
"That wasn't me," I said.
"Yeah, it was probably your twin brother. We were in
that two seat kayak, trying not to bother armed guards."
Perhaps I did have an identical twin brother.
That might explain why
this woman thought she knew me.
"I don't remember that at all," I confessed.
"That's what you said then too." She reached in
for a passionate kiss as if to convince me.
I didn't resist. She was attractive, this not Ann.
"Today a man showed me a card trick," she said.
She pulled a deck out of her bag and after shuffling
asked me to select a card, memorize it,
and put it back in the deck.
She then divided the deck into three piles
and then back again into one.

"What was your card?" she asked.
"I feel like I shouldn't tell you," I said.
She undid my cuff button
and rolled up the sleeve of my right arm.
There, on the inside of my forearm, was a tattoo
of the Queen of Hearts. I had no idea
how that got there. It was in fact my card.
"Most impressive," I noted.
She gave me that winning smile again.
"Did you bring the coupon?" she asked.
I checked my pockets. There were only my keys,
some loose change, a flash drive, and a newspaper article
someone had clipped out. I unfolded it
and gazed at the headline:
Man Lost At Sea In Caribbean Storm.
The article was about me. It described
everything I could remember about my past,
including my fine performance playing Tony
in a high school production of *West Side Story*.
"You were good as Tony," my female friend said.
"Yes, but I'm not dead," I told her.
"They think you are," she said, "but we know better."
I didn't know anything of the sort.
"Pinch me," I said, assuming that was the kind of test
that might prove worthwhile here.
"Maybe later," she said, "but we'd better get going
if we want to make that reservation."
I had all sorts of reservations, but as I watched her
get up and head down the street,
I found myself following after.

King of Aces

The magician was a sensitive soul,
kind and caring, a gift for attention to detail
that would serve him well in years
beyond when the magic ceased.
He was proud and confident then,
ever the showman, a fellow artist
working long hours at his specialized craft,
walking coins over knuckles, investing
necessary time to practice the dexterity
that ranked him among the world's best.
He invented one trick with four aces
that fooled them all, impressively, incredibly.
No one else knew how much it all mattered,
how hard he worked to make the close-up magic
seem effortless, chimerical, an embodiment
of madcap casual whimsy.
His friendship was a privilege,
watching him work a room illuminated
with the glowing spirit of reckless youth,
fueled by talent and ambition.
We traveled the back roads of Scotland,
entertaining lads and lasses nightly,
immune from the fears of an unknown future.
He was on the continent chasing down Skinner
in pursuit of promoting the idea of magic as therapy,
cards and coins hopeful of unlocking autistic cages,
in feats of semi-medicinal enchantment.
I wished him well, and went along for the ride,
playing second fiddle as indie musician,
while he won hearts and minds of strangers.
We reunited several years later, one New Year's morn,
climbing to the rooftop of a luxury Manhattan hotel,
his idea to go where no one was allowed, pushing
limits, thriving on this controlled danger,
for that was his way. I remember the view,
some sixty stories above the hung-over city,
forbidden, fearsome, and breathtaking.

The chill clear wind carried distant sounds
but mostly I heard the drumbeat of my own heart,
pumping excitement and the palpable thrill
of not knowing what happens next.

Jeremiad

The coterie of insiders
meets as though in divination,
trustees invoking corporate spirits
for some economic deus ex machina.
Their legerdemain is swift, skilled, subtle,
in marked contrast with the crude bombast
of the smiling CEO's confident message,
oversized yet simplified for the hungry masses.
They hide the bones of their conquests
in a cherry wood paneled charnel house,
and only the dust of decimation hints at
what has occurred. The sleight of hand is
anything but slight, as the mighty win again.

Those that have continue to get,
a relative constant Einstein failed to mention.
The trickle down, a soft rain as nature intended,
is expected but never arrives.
The rest go on dreaming, seeking to slake the thirst
to survive, parched and persistent, working
three jobs to make ends meet in this pretzel existence.
Wallowing in the opal moonlight, twisted phantoms
seek reparation, restitution, belated justice
in a harvest that proves barren fiction at best.
They follow rivers, battling currents,
bones off fighting to remain connected to life.

III. Assorted Wicks

Play

Camouflaged against orange and purple sunset,
we counted winking stars that swayed between branches
in smiling shadows of a flourishing summer's night.
Laying still there on our damp mattress of grass
we etched Leonardo's futuristic flying machines,
making connections amidst shared whispered revelations
that no civilized ruffian would ever hear,
feeding on the excitement of blind touch.

Anthem

It's always a question of vision in relation to light,
which seems to belabor the obvious, and yet we
quickly are hurled back to feelings of national pride
relative to the battered icon, a survivor's pleasure
that goes beyond hard proof of rockets, bombs,
and the spectacle and commotion that surrounds them.
Freedom and bravery are only but the start,
for three unknown verses continue unsung,
expanding, expounding upon the story.
From the shore, by a stream,
the silence is broken by a breeze which blows
in synchronistic concert with the morning's first rays
to great effect: the banner reflected in the water
overwhelms and delights. Pride, yes, but further
memories of confusion and the havoc of war,
the cleansing wash of dreaded enemy's blood,
from which there was no refuge. In triumph
a symbol waves, and may it ever be that freemen
stand in victory and peace, humbly preserved
by a higher power's grace and blessings,
that we answer in turn with trust and praise.
Today we take these lyrics in stride, neglecting
Key's happy reverence for that spangled field
of bright stars and broad stripes, instead reflecting
only our brash impatience to play ball
and somehow get on with the game.

Deluminate

That hipster nihilism
is a false conceit;
this is not Paris in the late '50s,
second-hand typewriters
clacking away like air-raid sirens
of some precocious world of art,
strange aperitifs the bold residuum
of late night contemplations
turned into philosophic bickering.
In those poetic times,
spontaneous flashes
would masquerade
as the offspring of Whitman,
and lesser beats
provided emotional rants,
love songs to the everyday
that were labeled profound.
Rediscovered Catullus ignited the senses
and Kerouac elevated and extended
the flow of ordinary conversation
to a shimmering reflection
of a romantic bay's city lights.
Words truly were king then,
and the frosty old man scoffed at
such rule breakers and
ne'er–do-wells.
Now suave pretenders
carry the mantle
of trendy toreadors,
stomping folk choruses
that presage tough times ahead,
busking homey messages
to charlatans and clowns
in disingenuous fashion.

Refrain

The unnecessary solo toward song's end
feels like a chapter out of place,
distinctive and echoing back upon itself,
hurried before time collapses.

The days repeat and lose meaning,
waiting out wishes granted, the promise
of past worlds dreamed, as unique
universes unfold in daunting ways.

It's all compiled in a gray anthology,
the basics of the modern,
rudiments of how things really are
before they grow in complication:

Categorized into stages, phases,
the shifting eras of an education,
flowing into careers and willful efforts.
All memories now, marked as mediocre.

Waiting for the light to turn, days
lengthen to announce seasonal change.
Expectation and revelation battle as ideas,
distinguished in solitary disappointment.

Finally, mesmerized by the ordinary,
it's a long breath bordered by silence.
This lingering all-time vision, that
pinions experience softly into place
and forms an idea called life.

Simile

You said I was like a bridge:
connecting things, strong.
I politely disagreed –
my foundations were far too weak.
Sure enough,
when she first tried to cross me,
I collapsed.

Prognosis

This was an awakening, a sitting up at attention
as you concentrate on directing spoon mouthward,
hoping some process of digestion will follow,
offering nutrition to this weary battle-tested vessel
attacked from within and without,
cells and chemicals and the gritty anguish of waiting.

This is the new wilderness, the grasping of concepts
that lead higher, further astray from the norm.
Watch your step, even as you fall.

And birds battle in treetops,
while the sun hangs heavy on the horizon,
an orange ball, a butterfly's flag
waving through a distant prism.

Seasons exchange names with slow progress,
a safeguard against radical change.
Give me the familiar whimper,
the rasping battle against pain
like a locomotive's plaintive cry
on its way to better places.

We are all on some intimate journey,
racing agendas and tourist attractions,
drawing in crowds like pollen-hungry bees.
You hide in plain sight, behind the notion
that normal might still be an option.

That lie comforts you, breathing
behind this mask of fantasy, an illusion
that tomorrow offers a promise
today's disappointment won't negate.
Twinkle, twinkle, wish away:
wish better, whisper and breathe,
then wish forevermore.

Signal Chain

1.
The fortune is apocryphal,
declaring her the sine qua non
of health and prosperity,
yet she finds the cookie
in a filthy shopping mall dumpster.

2.
She knows all the flatware pieces and
the proper place setting order, a sign
of good breeding, until the revelation
that mom stabbed dad with a salad fork,
and he fought back with a silver ladle.

3.
Having a troubled childhood doesn't go far
as currency in this foo barred society,
where fiascos are traded like pesos
at the border exchange mart, it's just a matter
of finding equivalencies, a mess of a mate.

4.
She's a restless sleeper, and when the son
of her father's business friend comes to
spend the night, she dreams he smothers the moon
in a paralyzing leg lock, showing no mercy.
In the morning, she doesn't tell him.

5.
Logic has no claim on matters of the heart,
and while she continues to look for omens
in the commonplace of her days, she also knows
that love can be strangely stoic, and that passion
often has a sour aftertaste, tumultuous and bitter.

Migration

When they came to arrest the woman,
you sat there, stone quiet,
a scabrous statue
pondering your own existence,
the shape of your navel,
the inability to smell your own breath,
and other trivialities of no real consequence.
Wishing you were different
never changed you yet.

She adored you once,
kept little pieces of paper
full of your clever witticisms
hidden in a shoebox in the back of her closet.
Then Australia separated you forever
and you lost your edge
and she vowed to not wear yellow again.

Our familial ties connect us
in ways our blood never quite did.
She looks at your old picture
and imagines your lips, your body,
in ways that real life never provided,
fulfilled through recurring drunken desire
and eventual moans of amazement.

Two birds flown off in separate directions
long ago
may never meet again.
Such is nature, these mirrors that reflect us,
such is life.

Gala

It is too easy, too simple to go ascribe blame,
but the fact is revealed in that we are weak,
chemically imbalanced mortal players,
reciting homilies to prior learning,
aches and hiding places and animal yearnings,
memories and more directed movements,
marking time like mirrors of celestial entities
orbiting our long night's imaginations.

You blend in foundation,
I shave familiar face that greets me.
We stare into the vacant realm together,
representing our respective genders,
friends, lives, and belongings, things
that comprise our so-called existence.
Shiny things reflect the light
and present us as we want to be seen.

The dance begins, another soul saved,
a charade of recovery and preaching to the choir.
Hours and holidays slip by like flowing water
and time and tide still rant impatiently.
Listen and you'll hear the faint susurrus,
the rasp of our folly, the alms of our aims.
It echoes in the snowstorm, winding through branches,
confiding in nature with what secrets remain.

Feathered Thing

It's mostly hearsay and conjecture,
but she could be available again
after a protracted and painful divorce,
so you would have to battle those ghosts
in addition to the ones you already share
from college days, and what seemed to
encompass a lifetime of promises unfulfilled.
She has taken good care of herself,
and this is no surprise. She always was
all about plans, the big picture, end results.
You were the damaged goods,
unrealized potential,
a jazz riff that ran on too long,
too tangentially.
That old relationship
was like striking out over and over again,
swinging for the fences and heading
back to the dugout, each time
embarrassed and somewhat confused.
So why does this news excite you,
stir ancient dreams, give life to the lie
of a happy ending, a sweet framed portrait
to put on the mantel next to the piano.
Futility has nothing on you,
and middle age makes
self-delusion run strong in the veins.
It courses hot when you see that
online photograph and get convinced
by the same smile that once punctuated
your daily existence into picking up
the phone and, contrary to smarter
common sense, starting what
cannot be stopped, letting
the phoenix of old passions prevail.

An Octave Apart

You and I are not so different.
To the untrained ear,
our stories are variations on a theme,
a melody left unresolved.
While one can refute
the merits of that chorus repeating,
a middle bridge that suspends
across the divides of divulged confession,
and lyrics that tell a powerful tale
of far too little and way too late,
there is one tune that plays on tonight,
wistful and whimsical, masking a doleful coda
that echoes regrets with a flurry of minor notes.
That is my song, and perhaps yours too,
interrupting the silence of others
with a musical statement at once majestic
and allegedly grand, yet perhaps more
imposition than composition to listeners astute.
The discordant truth is that most move on
with little more than a few clever notes
stuck in their heads, a momentary distraction
that fades as the next passionate phrase
comes along as replacement, a new refrain
for a different day. The harsh realization
that the world remains unmoved resonates,
while a universe rife with songs unsung
is the place where I choose to keep singing,
and, I expect, so will you.

Stasis

A breath is held
in hopes of stopping the onslaught.
This eyes closed shut fantasy
harbors a verge of expectation,
a glimmer of faith in the DNA
that progress is soon forthcoming.
The truth is a series of questions,
an exasperated sigh, a sad realization.
Like weather, the violence is here,
a daily occurrence:
uncommonly common
as sips soon become gulps,
glasses are emptied, skies darkened.
Hot it hits gullet, a reward
for random screaming.
The panic sets in;
names are mispronounced.
It's a medical condition
where all fades to black.
Smell this truth on my breath:
there is no catchphrase
to remedy our dilemmas.
We carry on, bravely ignorant,
hoping yet to survive.

None the Wiser

After your appointment as foreign secretary
our alumni mag published a short synopsis
of your impressive career trajectory,
an uncannily powerful, intelligent woman,
ever eager to give back to a desirous world.
It didn't mention
the long list of disposable friends,
and there was no residue of irony
in gracious quotes from peer associates.

Nobody called me.

I was an early consequence of
your fast tracked social growth,
some carnival detritus abandoned in haste,
behind the back of that double wide trailer.
I was your clown shoes, your loudly striped pants,
your embarrassing phase with reckless abandon,
a close brush with artistic independence.

You had me at hello.

From the cloistered hallways
of this fifth floor walkup studio
I choreograph my dreams
into expressive movements
designed to awake the limbic regions
of unsuspecting audience members.
The dust stirs; the music awakes
a certain maudlin sentimentality.

We have outgrown each other.

Those were your parting words,
long before your transfer,
your meticulous plan put into effect.
At every performance I scan the seats
looking for your face, embracing
inevitable disappointment, but
always scanning regardless.

Reconnaissance

It's never an easy explanation,
even while staring at twilight sky,
as sneakers of nearby joggers
beat rhythms into fading day.
You become reservoir for endless tales,
the rising level of excuses and alibis,
so-called reasons of avoidance to commitment
that threaten to drown a relationship.
You, the sedulous, meticulous, diligent opposition,
strive to keep a head above water,
reflecting rays of hope even when
moon stands in for sun and a sense
of déjà vu builds mountains of apprehension
against distant horizon.
You hear and interpret, sigh and reply,
follow script carefully,
never missing a beat,
even as the feeling arises again
that something big has passed you by.

Evolution

I sit on the plasticized seat,
ten yards from certain danger.
Beyond the near tracks, I can see
into someone's backyard,
a place where turtles might enjoy
the incessant commotion
as something that shakes things up in a lively way.
There is a dog tethered to a chain,
and some laundry hanging,
but little promise of real excitement,
the kind of heated overheard exchange
between secret lovers from an open window
that would compellingly punctuate
soundtrack of the Technicolor movie version.
This is suburbia, folks, and sometimes
the trains run late,
because life is unpredictable that way.
To prove this, the 8:20 express shows up
on the opposite side,
but we are not rattled.
We are pictures of adaptability.
Sure we groan and mumble,
but then as the swift vehicle
of our daily commute slows to allow for boarding,
we civilly turn and walk the extra few feet as
well-dressed brothers of polite mankind
that eagerly adjust to this new development,
proud survivors rolling toward a new horizon of change.

Onset

Don't you get it?
Cleo was a goldfish!
She romanticized time,
speaking of it as more than
an accounting,
a diary entry,
a personal journey,
as though it existed
outside genetic predisposition,
something tangential,
and equidistant to our
usual neighborhood haunts,
the underpass where
we walked our small dogs,
the creepy loneliness of
that sad podiatrist's office,
the convergence of avenues
where kickball games ruled.
I miss the brainteasers,
the unspoken competition,
the lazy afternoons,
the harmless taunting,
all in the service of childhood
fast transforming
into something else.

Hard Cycle

Like the sun rising yellow
over rows of burgeoning lavender,
you give me a farmer's hope,
the endless optimism
of a successful growing season to come,
the sweet reminders – rows of red tulips
like well drawn lipstick lines
against distant horizon.
We are blessed in this beauty
and a silo full of hopes,
canopied in solitude like a pale aspen forest,
and here in nuanced corners
of the pine-needle carpet,
moss will smooth hard edges over,
serving up the lushly soft perspective
on nature's often harsh measures,
creeping over rock and fallen timber,
pulling a blanket over napping scenery,
until such time as a harvest season
fuels another hard-working celebration.

Surmising the Situation

A mountain of bedclothes,
long curtains drawn anonymously,
detritus of a playful night.
Room service tray
like playful set piece,
reflecting quarter moon,
catching rays as if
calling to all sorts of appetite.

Delight's doppelgänger,
your abandoned clothes
suggesting poses to the mind's eye,
inner desires revealed,
insatiable nymph,
or the agonizing realization
you might be here against your will.

Depending on inner judgments
or social classifications
or what is truly found within;
I am not the one you'd imagined
when imagining was done.

(You are the ultimate arbiter,
Lady Justice wielding her blind sword,
rent through, I am the one
struck by your sharp dangers,
bending beside you, unable
to resist the challenge
of surviving this madness,
gazing into your closed eyes,
and knowing you feel the same
even as you lie here, quietly breathing.)

The Reveal

You are the waif, the wastrel,
the soot-faced urchin of some ancient Dickens tale,
hands outstretched in subtle supplication,
seeking assistance with the practiced innocence
of a seasoned charmer, short skirt and long legs
working a discrete incantation, luring in
and mesmerizing, distracting from the descending
and pervasive cloud of leaden sadness.
The day is heavy with possibility,
hot with humid expectation, palpable and hyper-real.
Without sound and from a great distance,
this could be someone's paradise.
Up close, though,
beads of sweat attack cosmetic touch-ups,
pathos and desperation suck the sweet vitality
from this dog day and the music of your little voice
turns acidic, astringent, atonal.
Appalling long shadows
(and what they reveal)
ultimately claim
another summer's pyrrhic victory.

Party Favors

The dress color's faded,
the spirit seems wrung over
by too many lost battles.
So she feigns indifference,
stays off by herself,
quietly praying to a darker god.
He finds her genuflecting,
drawn by intensity,
overcome by blue eyes.
This is her fiery tagline,
the very same one she rues,
shellacked surface
of apathy as polite disclaimer,
hiding a host of telling cracks.
The night is polished
with stars reflecting secrets,
and shiny individual scars,
each with a frightening
yet compelling narrative
saying this world's a cruel place
and here's the hard proof.
He cannot escape the smile,
the whippoorwill's sad call,
this endless patch of night.

Illuminated

The late shadow in the lea
is uneven, disjointed, wrong.
Birds no longer sound like birds.

The summer light is fickle, unpredictable.
It skips whole meals and toys with clouds.
It shows up and says it wants you back.

The light catches your eye.
Napping on the daybed, you are caught:
dreams exposed for all to see.

The sun whispers at dawn,
then sings its way through breakfast,
something about being taken lightly,

with a chorus about burning desire.
The agile sprinter crosses the sky
and disappears reluctantly.

Theorists always predict a tomorrow,
but summer light reserves its right
to playfully surprise you. Again.

IV. Shadow Tricks

Invasive

The silver creek at sunset,
the scintillating sense of summer's distinguished swath
against otherwise mundane country coloring,
a hint of elegance, of riches nature hides below.
Crisp fresh mountain air, furrows of melted ground ice,
the remnants of hope that harken back to simpler times
of purity, innocence, so little of this remains
trickling through mossy roots of ancient grasses,
Spanish heath, seaside daisy, lantana,
the whole of blue mountain bushland,
acacia balleyana's yellow dance, joined by
coreopsis laneolata's orange smile,
ipomoea indica's lavender invitation,
red berries of leycesteria formosa,
or white butterfly flowers of
creeping tradescantia fluminensis.

He steps gingerly through the vinca,
thinking of his lover's body back when
first they went camping:
that early morning shower, that tiny tent,
the unexpected beauty of her nakedness
wrapped only in a sleeping bag's insulation.
It was a time of goodness and exploration,
wondering about meanings of nature's signals,
trying to learn names of all they found there,
young and unable to interpret things,
feelings, the glory of identification,
the impossibility of control.

Seasons of Loss

Sirens clear the streets
in money city, where
side alleys are like circuitous veins
in search of pumping heart.
There's no time for debating demerits,
so many go along for the ride.
Moments exist for each event:
confession, confrontation, repentance,
a new investment.
The pointlessness evokes
a uniquely nervous laughter,
and a desire to make future plans.
Rendezvous at the usual places
and regret how the weekend
always ends too soon.
Routines beget habit:
happy days are here again,
frequent customer cards are punched,
and yet it still costs more.
Life as souvenir,
words as evidence,
and a debit sheet that proves
the foolishness of
buying on margin.
Consider the long term
as if a given,
but the mournful notes
dying on the afternoon breeze
remind us otherwise.
Risk and reward
are not allies always,
and past results
are no guarantee
for antiquated dreams.

Back to School

The calendar page turns
from the dog days of August,
to a September unlike any other.
We grieve the department colleagues
chosen to give up this worldly journey
these past few months,
suddenly,
shockingly,
for reasons unfathomable.

The long days of summer were broken up
by wakes and funerals, harsh reminders
of mortality, that beauty and humor and
sweet generosity of spirit is always a limited deal,
except in memories where they live on,
vibrant,
resonant,
vital.

That first meeting we share fond stories
of these missing comrades,
and once again tears flow freely.
The hallways are strangely silent
without their friendly voices,
their knowing smiles,
their seasoned sayings of advice
that kept us all on even keel.

The year itself is cast with shadows,
and an ongoing optimism that
with each new school day
will come a happy realization
that this was all a crazy dream.
But after all, it was not.
And still school bells ring,

days broken into discrete periods
of instruction, yet the largest lesson
cannot be taught, it is the one
forever marked by their absence.

Happenstance

The beauty of uncertainty
is part of the allure,
the faces look familiar,
yet a million times unsure.
The voices clamor destiny,
a resonance of chance.
Push and pull, eventually,
one learns this foreign dance.
The signs resist interpreting,
coincidence and fate,
the plot marries the setting here,
the seasons match the date.
A hint is dropped, a verbal cue,
and so the world begins:
two strangers, not a single clue,
and seven deadly sins.

Not for Us

The tenor and timbre are similar
whether form response or personal:
they speak of appreciating the chance
to read, reread and carefully consider,
but these aren't quite right,
they are not a good fit,
in short, they are not for us.
Best wishes are sent
in sending stuff elsewhere
and thanks extended
for the trust implicit
in choosing this journal or contest.
The backlog caused this delay,
and you have our apologies,
but please wait a month before submitting again.
They are messages of regret,
of numerical odds working against you,
of bad timing or fickle fate,
of clashing aesthetics or
the planets being poorly aligned.
Sometimes it's not about the work,
for politics exist in the smallest arenas,
and personal visions and
mercurial temperaments
often rule the day.
This is the moment of discouragement,
denied even the decency of some account
why your work has been declined.
Is it better to hear that these works
would be improved by greater concision
or more original language,
that while your message is inspirational
your words are prosaic, your syntax disjointed,
your rhythm unregulated?
Are you better for knowing
you lack an emotional point of access,
that such emotions seem disembodied
or overly sentimental,

the action too static and rife
with clichéd assertions,
that there is redundancy,
too much formality,
or not enough?
The language is underspecified,
or possibly too abstract.
Yet your words are lovely things.
No doubt they will find suitable homes
in short order. Our loss, they say,
much luck and hope you continue to prosper.
But for now, it's a no,
So good luck dealing
with this temporary setback.

Unnatural Law

Well into the sinecure of her summer,
she looks for amusements,
laying subtle triggers
bound to snag one far less aware,
more likely to stumble against the power
of that raw disquisition, her proclaiming
the rules of relationship regulation
as if stating scientific fact.
His response is supplication,
an argument against limits,
a plea for heightened engagement,
a celebration of their unity
prior to the inevitable parting.
She takes a parenthetical tone,
cautionary and unyielding.
He shows her a heart on fire,
a playlist keen to enflame and incite,
to pluck sensation from memory
and spark it to reanimation.
But she is keen to sever the connection,
to allay the fantods haunting her dreams,
to get on with the rest of her life.
Under slick guise of sincerity,
she sweetly explains that sooner beats later,
that there's no reward in waiting for eventual pain.
He lies there after, prostrate,
not quite hearing the words right in his mind,
all echoes and reverb, modulated nonsense
that tricked him into misery as maturation,
a death match of emotion versus reason.

Prophet

The sidewalks were his daily agenda,
the park bench his summer accommodation.
And when tourists and city denizens
stroll by with equal measures disregard and disgust,
he lets them know about the secret messages
found by reading every third word of the road signs
on the interstates, how they reveal the catalysts
and clues to the impending alien invasion.
Your highfalutin ignorance sickens me, he tells them,
as they cut a wide swath to try and ignore
this man whose odor announces his proximity
long before any conspiracy theory ever does.
The breeze wafts all this information upward
and carries it to the corners of the nearby cathedral.
Soon the days will grow shorter again
and he will take his mission elsewhere,
racing to reach the populace ahead of the fateful event,
before they come to erase his mind
again.

Anagnorisis

Rules can save lives,
but you must learn to read
between given lines.

Maps are the same way.
Let me chart your points
and touch your topography.

I will tread your insets,
feel the key to reading
your inner thoughts to scale.

I see your reasons for revenge,
understand your raging anger,
empathize the depths of this betrayal.

It is not wise to incur your wrath
and this is made plain up front.
You do not hide emotions well.

I'll sing an ode for reason,
for quieter contemplation
where cooler heads yet prevail.

It is small consolation, agreed,
but rash actions may also
anger the often-fickle gods.

Forget the past as prologue.
I can give you safe harbor,
provided you see I am no clown.

You, skilled woman of reason,
can interpret the obscure oracle:
You can provide for my needs.

Together we can shock a waiting world
if you join me in that foreign place
where rules are mapped out clearly.

Second Act

Twenty years ago, she had performed in his one-act play
"The Kiss," off Broadway, now he was meeting her train
at noon. She greets him with hug and kiss, as fashion
dictates, in a smart black dress. The amazing station
is filled with lunchtime stragglers, people whose love
is transformed into browsing shops with an empty

sense, on the hunt for that which they'd gladly empty
wallets if shopping fancy is struck or they'll still play
at this hour's game of restless contemplation, where love
is not a factor. For these two, they talk of her train
ride, the anniversary, wheeling like stars on the station
ceiling, floating satellites reunited when, after a fashion,

their orbits happily realign. She had been a fashion
designer, feted as a visionary mogul, but fame felt empty
so she danced away. She'd opted for a change of station,
choosing a farmer in Provence, a conservative play
compared to husbands prior. She was keen to train
him, but first she escaped to meet with an old love.

In a park, watching vagrants and birds, she asked, "Love,
why were we never a couple?" He couldn't fashion
an answer. "Bad timing," he said, "just two trains
heading opposite directions." She accepted this empty
wisdom. Even when she had starred in his play,
those trains had long since left the station.

Life molded discrete fates. When the radio station
played the song that once inspired visions of love,
all they mustered were smiles. Decades ago, he'd played
that song, a sad rendition sung in coffeehouse fashion
in hopes of eliciting a night together. That empty
hope grew into friendship, the kind you couldn't train

others to have, the kind that inspired taking a long train
ride to see her soul-mate. Soon, it's back to the station

and real life, new husband, and all the echoes of empty dreams must be filed away another time. "Our love transcends time," she says, boarding in graceful fashion. "Yes," he says, to a kiss he'd once captured in a play.

He watched her train depart, distantly separating love from love again, leaving him empty at the station, fashion designer fading like lines from a long-ago play.

Lex Loci

It's a polylemma, she says,
aware that not one person
in the Costco warehouse
knows what she means.
And you consumers are the linchpin!
She likes to lecture others,
especially while getting free samples
of hot food all the while.
It's all the attention she gets.
At one time, she still had big dreams
of splendiferous munificence,
she of the hilltop mansion,
wealthy and philanthropic,
sending off checks
to do her good deeds for her.
Now reality screams
that she missed her chances,
squandered a spectrum
of remote but possible opportunities,
and instead let time run rampant
like an out-of-control toddler,
messing up the well-placed toys
of careful plans, leaving her
befuddled, bedraggled,
faded and funky and
more than a little bit sad.
She is the bag of giblets,
the one that you know is there,
yet must be removed
before progress ensues,
the one no one cares about,
deserted and misunderstood.
She proceeds to the express line
and points out to all within earshot
that the sign *should* say 15 items or *fewer.*
Welcome to America, she mutters,
while others go about their days.

Submerged

There's nowhere else to go.
I am a long subway ride away,
even after discarding my unrealistic vision
of who you might be.
You entertain on cruise ships
for people who cannot appreciate your talent.
As they blindly applaud, you know
you are in the middle of an ocean.
You get propositions from waiters
caught in a holding pattern.
Everyone is a bundle of potential,
but few bundles ever get unpacked.
You know this now. You are on board,
having experienced strange sinking feelings.
All those years of training. All the laughs,
those alcoholic concoctions consumed in haste,
all those meals bought in expectation of favors.
It's become habit, like snoring, breaking down,
or trying to breathe. Inhale and start the
next movement carefully, adagio,
because these bright lights only last for so long.

Underpass

We sit there staring,
isolated from the world,
cars racing by at speeds
far beyond posted limit.
Yet we don't see them,
we only hear the echo of the roar
as another sixteen-wheeler
passes en route to a distant
point of important delivery.
We consort, consider the
mystery cargo, its need for
refrigeration, the perfect
comfort of our silence.
I block thoughts of how
this spot is mere yards away
from where my father went down
that morning, suddenly made aware
of a faulty heart needing
surgical repair, assistance.
Instead I watch the meaningless
passing of speeding vehicles,
and think kindly of you,
pretty you, the coincidences
that drove us together,
the roar of my heart
when we kiss, not ever
dreaming how, a few years later,
I'd be the one driving you
to unforgivable tears.

Reins

The wind carries hints of sharp spice and dung,
and those who listen extra carefully
hear remnants of ringing manjiras,
singing mirrored motions of exotic gyrations,
stoking the arterial fire, boiling blood
with lust and wanton desire, lost
in a whorl of sensual overload
in a world that does not allow
true release or free expression.
Rather, the marketplace is chockablock
with strident morning bidders, hagglers vying
for a prime cut of meat, a ripened fruit,
a succulent way to overcome the boundaries
of tradition, sacrifice, and solemn vows
that war with nature's sweet urgings,
to vent pent-up frustration at the long table
through comestible comfort in this odd land
of atavistic and revolutionary indifference.

Queen of Period Eight

She makes a volcano in lab, and I dream of her
for a month after. Chasing through fields of wheat,
eager to touch that purple velour top.
She is my special harvest, the one I have
watched sprout from seeds and watering and sun.

I have never been to her house, but I
can describe her room, the way everything
is perfectly in its assigned place, grouped by colors,
textures, systematically labeled by genus,
inviting my eventual invasion.

She is sheltered; orthodontic braces
protecting that innocent smile from a harsh world.
Her laugh is a sweet giggle, a hiccup of
mirth that spills down from the heavens
whenever I playfully appease her.

When I catch her in the field,
I know it is only because she lets me.
She folds me in quarters, and puts
me away on her closet shelf,
on top of pink floral contact paper,
and I go gladly into the darkness,
knowing she will someday return.

Her bed is stacked full with dolls
of many nations, silent girls
in native dress with mysterious expressions
who share her quiet friendship
with comfort and pride. From them,
I learn my place.

Life is impermanent,
a parade of clothing and furniture
that grows tired over passing seasons.
She is a beaker of solution, a careful notation,
and my heart ignites like Bunsen's burner,
a steady and useful flame that I know
is necessary for results currently sought.

Greatest Fan

Sight unseen, I know you well,
like some silent film soundtrack,
so when I hear laughter erupt
from across the crowded room,
I know you are the cause,
your abundant personality
mixing wit and charm into
a spirited effort of will.

I know that in the second reel
you leave with another,
some nameless young heartthrob,
athletically designed to invoke
the infamous green-eyed monster.
When the laughs dissipate into
frayed threads of tired conversation,
patterns reveal exhaustion,
conventions indicating nothing more
than revisionist history.

In the end it's another remake,
same story with an updated twist.
Top down, pedal to the floor,
there's another fade to black
and credits that never roll
the way one might hope to see.
Ever the loyalist, I stay,
watching to the very last,
long after everyone has gone
and the lights rise on sad reality.

www.ingramcontent.com/pod-product-compliance
Lightning Source LLC
Chambersburg PA
CBHW071531080526
44588CB00011B/1632